GINA M. EMANUEL-SATCHELL

THE DANCE MINISTER
AND
DANCE TECHNIQUE

WHAT GOD SAYS ABOUT SKILL

Copyright © 2023 Gina M. Emanuel-Satchell

Scripture quotations marked (Amp) are taken from the AMPLIFIED® BIBLE, Copyright© 1954, 1958, 1962, 1964, 1965, 1987 by the Lockman Foundation Used by Permission. (www.Lockman.org). Scripture quotations taken from the Amplified® Bible (AMPC), Copyright © 1954, 1958, 1962, 1964, 1965, 1987 by The Lockman Foundation Used by permission. lockman.org".Scripture quotations marked (BSB) are taken from The Holy Bible, Berean Study Bible, (BSB) Copyright ©2016, 2020 by Bible Hub Used by Permission. All Rights Reserved Worldwide.https://bereanbible.com Scripture quotations marked (ESV) are taken from THE HOLY BIBLE, ENGLISH STANDARD VERSION®, Copyright© 2001 by Crossway, a publishing ministry of Good News Publishers. Used by permission. Scripture quotations marked (MSG) are taken from THE MESSAGE, copyright © 1993, 2002, 2018 by Eugene H. Peterson. Used by permission of NavPress, represented by Tyndale House Publishers. All rights reserved. Scripture quotations marked (NASB) are taken from the NEW AMERICAN STANDARD BIBLE®, Copyright© 1960, 1962, 1963, 1968, 1971, 1972, 1973, 1975, 1977, 1995 by The Lockman Foundation. Used by permission.Scripture quotations marked (NIV) are taken from THE HOLY BIBLE, NEW INTERNATIONAL VERSION®. Copyright© 1973, 1978, 1984, 2011 by Biblica, Inc.™. Used by permission of Zondervan. Scripture quotations marked (NKJV) are taken from the NEW KING JAMES VERSION®. Copyright© 1982 by Thomas Nelson, Inc. Used by permission. All rights reserved. Scripture quotations marked (NLT) are taken from the Holy Bible, New Living Translation, copyright ©1996, 2004, 2015 by Tyndale House Foundation. Used by permission of Tyndale House Publishers, Carol Stream, Illinois 60188. All rights reserved.Scripture quotations marked (WEB) are taken from the WORLD ENGLISH BIBLE, public domain. No part of this document may be reproduced or transmitted in any form or by any means, electronic, mechanical, photocopying, recording, or otherwise, without prior written permission of the author.

THE DANCE MINISTER AND DANCE TECHNIQUE
WHAT GOD SAYS ABOUT SKILL

Gina M. Emanuel-Satchell
smoothstonedance@gmail.com

ISBN 978-1-949826-65-4

Printed in the USA.
All rights reserved

Published by: EAGLES GLOBAL BOOKS | Frisco, Texas
In conjunction with the 2023 Eagles Authors Course
Cover & interior designed by DestinedToPublish.com

DEDICATION

My Mother – Dr. Alice Mercedes Colón-Lacey

My mother is one of the most hardworking and career-driven women I have ever known. I have seen her return to school to get her GED, obtain her bachelor's degree, continue to receive her master's degree, and finally obtain a doctorate
– all majoring in psychology.

My mother has been through a lot in her lifetime, starting with her childhood, but she persevered and pressed her way through to accomplish her dreams. I know it wasn't easy, but I know it was worth it for her in the end. She is a reminder to me that despite all I have gone through in my life, and continue to go through, I can also persevere. I will continue to press my way through until I have reached my dreams.

A fond memory I have is when I won the Miss Pennsylvania, "Hal Jackson's Talented Teens" talent pageant in 1979, where I traveled with and was chaperoned by the pageant coordinator to Los

Angeles, California. My mom flew and met me out there so that she could be in the audience to cheer me on. I was so happy!

Thanks, Mom. I love you.

My Father – Arthur Nathaniel Satchell Sr.

5/8/1939 – 3/9/2022

My father was the first man I have ever loved. He came into my life when I was a toddler, adopted me, and gave me his last name. He moved our family to Philadelphia, Pennsylvania, to give us a good life, and he did just that. I will forever be grateful for a man who can father children who do not naturally belong to him and taking them as his own is the most loving and selfless thing to do. I am ever grateful for all that he taught me.

A memory I treasure is after one of my dance recitals while leaving the event, I was wearing my tutu and carrying flowers, and Dad so proudly stopped traffic just so I could walk across Broad Street in Philadelphia, which is a wide and busy street. I loved that!

I love you and miss you, Dad.

SPECIAL DEDICATION

The greatest part of me and the people I love the most are my heartbeats – my children:

Ebonee Lee Emanuel, Jeffrey Howard Emanuel II, and Raven Nicole Emanuel.

PREFACE

I went to Saint Athanasius Catholic School in Philadelphia, Pennsylvania, as a child, and when I was in approximately the fifth grade, one of the nuns (Sister Mark) asked me if I wanted to participate in the Easter play. After I agreed, she told me to go home and ask my mother to buy ballet slippers, because she was going to teach me "a dance."

I met with Sister Mark after school, and she taught me a dance to the song "I Don't Know How to Love Him" from the Broadway play *Jesus Christ Superstar*. This was a song about Mary Magdalene, and how Jesus changed her life, and she finally knew what true love was. She turned out to be one of Jesus' greatest disciples! The dance involved me washing Jesus' feet, and after the play was over, I fell in love with dance immediately and asked my mother if I could go to dance school. I danced throughout grade school and attended the High School for Creative and Performing Arts (CAPA) in Philadelphia, and I also danced as a young adult.

I stopped dancing for many years and spent time being a wife and raising my three children. In the late 90's, I moved to Springfield,

Massachusetts, and rededicated my life to the Lord. I joined a church where the pastor's wife found out that I was a dancer and dance teacher. She asked if I would be interested in participating in a Resurrection Day presentation by ministering in dance. I agreed, and she told me that she wanted me to be Mary Magdalene and wash Jesus' feet! The look that I gave her... all I knew was I had the same exact experience as a child. After I ministered in dance that year, I never stopped.

I don't think it was a coincidence that I was asked to do the very same dance, portraying the very same biblical character, for the very same purpose. God reminded me that I did not do my first dance in a dance studio or on a stage – the art of dance was introduced to me in a church, and my very first dance was done on an altar. On the altar is where dance began for me, and the altar is where my dance belongs.

I have been called to help and assist by teaching dance techniques to the dance minister to enhance the gift God has already given them. If I can assist with providing more structure to their bodies, which can produce more confidence, it will help the dance minister to focus less on the technique and more on the worship.

CONTENTS

Dedication i
Special Dedication iii
Preface v
Forward ix
Note From The Author xi
Introduction xiii

Chapter 1
God Knows My Heart 1

Chapter 2
It's Not About the Technique, It's About the Passion 12

Chapter 3
Dance Should Only Be Done Spontaneously by the Holy Spirit 22

Chapter 4
I Tried Taking a Technique Class and I Don't Like It 33

Chapter 5
I Don't Need Technique Classes 42

Chapter 6
I Am Not Trying to Be a Technical Dancer 51

Chapter 7
There Are No (Adult) Classes in My Area 60

Chapter 8
I Don't Want to Learn from 'XYZ' 67

Chapter 9
Waiting to Go Only to the Conference/Workshop
XYZ Is Teaching At... 76

Chapter #10
XYZ Is a Dance Teacher in Our Ministry,
but We Don't Use Him/Her... 82

Epilogue 91
References... 94
Endorsement 96
Acknowledgments 98
Special Acknowledgment... 100

FORWARD

I first met Gina Emanuel-Satchell when she came to me as a student at the Eagles International Training Institute. I knew from the first time we talked that she has a tremendous knowledge of her God-given gift of movement. Her experience as a dancer, teacher, and choreographer proves that she is someone others can learn from and look up to as a mentor and role model. Her voice is relevant and important, and she is willing to share her many years of expertise, as she has done in *The Dance Minister and Dance Technique: What God Says About Skill*. As she shares her heart, I know the reader will be strengthened, challenged, and encouraged. The knowledge shared in this book provides both insight and revelation on how to think beyond the norm to press toward the high calling of God in Christ Jesus. As one who has served in the ministry of dance for over 25 years, I found this book to be important for the beginning minister of dance as well as for the seasoned minister. Not only did the book bless me, but it stirred up a new fire and a new passion within my heart.

The Dance Minister and Dance Technique: What God Says About Skill answers many questions that dance ministers face at some point in their ministry. The reader will be equipped to have a clean heart before God, serve others with humility, and minister in excellence. With the turn of every page of this book, the reader will find wisdom, tools, and ideas to grow in their assignment and to develop their gifts to their highest capacity. I highly recommend this read to all dance ministers. It will be a great study for dance ministry teams. It is clear that Gina has a heart for the dance minister to see the importance of being equipped and to have the necessary tools to be able to equip others so each minister can effectively fulfill their purpose in ministering to God's people through the gift of dance.

Apostle Pamela Scott Hardy, D.Min.
Founder, Eagles International Training Institute
The Eagles Network
Eagles Nest International Center

NOTE FROM THE AUTHOR

Being anointed means being empowered from on high – we carry God's Spirit, and we minister to encourage others and empower them to prosper in everything they do. The anointing should remove burdens (heaviness) and destroy the yokes (rope from around the neck) of bondage (no freedom); people should be healed and set free through our anointed movements.

We can dance technically and still be inspired by the Holy Spirit. Is the Holy Spirit limited by technique, or does adding technique deter us from the Holy Spirit? Absolutely not! Remember, dance technique is the process of taking care of our bodies and working on improving our movement. Learning dance techniques assists us with how to carry our bodies and how we center ourselves, which helps us with our rhythm and flow. Those who are committed to dancing for the Lord should be committed to perfecting the gift of dance that God has given us.

Technique training enhances our passion and our love for the Lord, and it does not mean taking a class will take away that passion. It's all about taking those moves rooted out of our passion, ingrained with the movement of the Holy Spirit and utilizing technical skills to help us with our confidence, poise, grace, stamina, balance, and core strength. By doing this and developing our dance skills, God will be pleased, because we are taking the time to enhance the gift, become more skillful, and dance more in excellence for Him.

In His Service.
Minister Gina M. Emanuel-Satchell

INTRODUCTION

God gave us our lives and the free will to do what we want in this life. Within that scope, we must realize that, yes, this is our life, but we must also remember that God gave us our lives (our bodies) and we are not our own – we have been bought with the blood of Jesus.

> *"Don't you realize that your body is the temple of the Holy Spirit, who lives in you and was given to you by God? You do not belong to yourself, for God brought you with the high praise. So you must honor God with your body."* – 1 Corinthians 6:19-20 (NLT)

This is not a book about trying to make people do things they don't want to do, but more about helping to open their eyes, being encouraging, and shedding light on investing time in what we love – dance. We should want to do and be better by doing what God wants us to do and being the very best that we can be. God has given us talents and gifts that we use in our everyday lives, and what we do with those talents and gifts should be done unto the Lord. God has asked us to do things decently and in order: to strive, to flow, and to function in excellence. God always gives us what we need, and He gives us His very best, so shouldn't we give Him our very best?

Our talents and gifts are something we are born with (naturally), but skill is something that we work at and build (technically). Yes, God can use anyone – skilled or unskilled – to do things for Him, but when God had specific assignments, He was looking to use a person of skill. When David was preparing for the Ark of the Covenant in Jerusalem, he sought out a skilled musician by the name of Kenaniah, who he made the choir director. David did not select singers who were just okay or who had no talent; he wanted the very best-skilled musician to present the best worship to the Lord. Mediocre was not what David looked for, and mediocre is not what God should receive.

> *"Now David was clothed in a robe of fine linen, as were all the Levites who were carrying the ark, and as were the musicians, and Kenaniah, who was in charge of the singing of the choirs. David also wore a linen ephod."* – 1 Chronicles 15:27 (NIV)

David was chosen by God for an important assignment, and he needed skilled people for an anointed event. Even his garments had to be of excellent fabric and quality. So God expects nothing less from us, and He wants people who are skilled to accomplish His assignments. Not only is skill important when ministering, but we must worship God in Spirit and in truth, and He wants us to worship Him in excellence. God wants us to take our passion, talent, and gift, and to work and develop our skills to worship Him with bodies that are prepared and strengthened.

In my observations over the years, as well as conversations with other dance leaders and ministers, I have been really perplexed by the following:

- The musician will individually work on his/her talent and gift by practicing or taking lessons, to be prepared to meet with the rest of the worship team, so that the chords, beats, and rhythm blend in unison when they play together.
- The singer/vocalist will practice individually to strengthen his/her vocal cords, in preparation for practicing with the worship singers, to sing in harmony and blend in unison.
- However, when it comes to the dancers, some will take technique classes, and some will not.

If classes aren't available or aren't attainable, then regular attendance at dance workshops and conferences are options. Another option is if there is an individual who has technique training on your dance ministry team, the technique can be incorporated into the curriculum during dance rehearsals or Bible study time.

When dance ministers take time to invest in their gift of movement, whatever they learn individually, they can bring to the group/team and work together corporately. The dance minister/team should put forth the same effort as the other worship artists/ministers. Dancing must be more than just a hobby when utilizing it as a gift in the house of God. Why not make us more prepared and better at the gift God already has given us by improving our dance skills and becoming more effective as dancers and dance ministers? If the other worship artists can take time to work on their skills, then why not the dance minister?

In the chapters ahead, I will be sharing the reasons, or "excuses," I have learned of or heard for why dance ministers will not invest time in taking dance technique classes or utilizing technically trained dancers. As I reveal what I have heard or seen, and what has been shared with me, my hope is to reveal – and hopefully help the dance minister see – the importance of being skilled, and what God has to say about it.

CHAPTER 1

GOD KNOWS MY HEART

What is a heart? In the natural, as stated by the Cleveland Clinic, "your heart is the main organ of your cardiovascular system; a network of blood vessels that pumps blood throughout your body. It also works with other body systems to control your heart rate and blood pressure. It is the primary organ of your entire circulatory system."[1] Without your heart, you cannot live. It is the very center and core of your being.

An article on the Everlasting Strength website states something very interesting about the heart:

> Cardiology is the branch of medicine that deals with diseases and abnormalities of the human heart. In the Bible the heart is mentioned 987 times and almost all of these refer to our spiritual heart… The Great Commandment is to love God with all our hearts (Matthew 22:37-38). This makes "spiritual Cardiology" very important in our lives. One of the most important things in all of Scripture is to have a healthy heart. But what exactly is our spiritual "heart"? Before we can study the heart and "heart disease," we need to understand the structure and function of

our spiritual hearts. This will enable us to properly listen to our hearts and diagnose any problems so that God can provide healing and spiritual "medicine."[2]

When I minister in dance, I put my whole heart and soul into it and worship with liberty and freedom – God is my heartbeat. I spend time being intimate with Him in prayer and meditation, and we have a love affair because He knows me, and I seek Him; this is called the heart of intimacy. I have ministered in dance in churches and at various events, and I have choreographed others to minister. Over the years, I have heard from people that there was something different about my dance or choreography and they were moved, or the movements were so prophetic, and it ministered to them. I even had a person tell me they were inspired to dance in their prayer closet at home. I said to them all, "Glory to God – it is all Him!" (That is, it is not me, but God who moves through me.) What they were seeing was the heart of worship. The time we spend with God in the secret place will shape our understanding of who God is, and what we pour into our spirit will reveal our true spiritual heart – a heart after God.

By the Spirit, it is God's heart that pumps His Word into our lives, and He is the reason *"we live and move and have our being"* (Acts 17:28 NIV). When we let the arteries of our hearts open to allow His blood to pump through us, only then can He be the center and core of our being by the Spirit. We must have the mind of Christ and know His thoughts before we speak or *move*. When we say, "God knows our heart," are those words that God spoke to us, or are those words we say to people when they talk to us about taking dance technique training?

Remember, out of the abundance of our heart our mouth speaks, and what we say, we will have (Matthew 12:34). If we are not saying what God says and the words are not coming from Him, that is our flesh. It is hard to believe that one would consult with the Lord about such a subject, and He would say, "You don't need that, because I know your heart." Our hearts must be aligned with His, and if it's something that is going to edify and teach us, and it's part of our ministry unto God, why would He say that?

Did He really tell you that, and did you consult with Him about it?

_____

_____

"Trust in the Lord with all your heart; do not depend on your own understanding. Seek his will in all you do, and he will show you which path to take." – Proverbs 3:5-6 (NLT))

God indeed knows our hearts; in fact, He knows everything there is to know about us. He knows every hair on our head and our every thought; God even knows the end from the beginning! He knows all and sees all – our past and our future. God gave us our lives to live, and He is expecting us to live it well, as unto Him.

We must also remember that the heart is part of our flesh, which is sinful by nature, and it cannot lead us. The Word of God must lead us, and it is what He has to say about our lives. We should be very careful that our hearts do not deceive us, because the Holy Spirit can be telling us one thing, and our hearts may say something else. So it is important that we stay in tune with God through prayer so we can hear from Him and discern when it is a matter of our hearts or His heart. Yes, we are human, and God gave us our emotions, but we must make sure we are maintaining our emotions and can discern when our hearts are right, and when we need to go back to our prayer closet. There is so much power and revelation in prayer.

> *"The heart is deceitful above all things, and desperately sick; who can understand it? 'I the Lord search the heart and test the mind, to give every man according to his ways, according to the fruit of his deeds.'" - Jeremiah 17:9-10 (ESV)*

When it comes to matters of the heart, it is God's heart that we seek, and before we can even consider ministering in dance, our relationship with Him must be solid. We must have a firm foundation in the Word of God and spend time with Him to hear what His heart is saying. Dance ministers cannot use the phrase "God knows my heart" as a reason for not seeking out training in dance technique; it is, unfortunately, an excuse.

An excuse is defined as "a reason put forward to conceal the real reason for an action; a pretext."[3] An excuse is not honored by the Lord, because it is a decision made by a sinful heart (flesh). If we as dance ministers truly know the heart of the Father, we will know that downplaying an opportunity to improve our skill and minimizing dancers who have technique is not the Father's heart. We can pursue and implement technique as part of our skill process, and it will not take away from our Father's heart; it can bring us closer to it! Our heart must be the Father's heart, and the heart of God is the heart of worship, one that worships Him in Spirit and in truth.

> *"But when the Friend comes, the Spirit of the Truth, he will take you by the hand and guide you into all the truth there is. He won't draw attention to himself but will make sense out of what is about to happen and, indeed, out of all that I have done and said."* – John 16:13 (MSG)

Excuses are reasons to fail, and we can stop ourselves from going forth in doing things that we just might be capable of. We should not be quick to give up without trying, because excuses can be derived from being insecure, a lack of confidence, or disliking something or someone, and not being truthful about it.

If we are insecure, then that simply means we are not secure in our decisions, capabilities, or skills. It's like being behind a wall and literally holding it up, not letting it fall, for fear of what's behind it. We need to have something to hold on to, and while we are doing this, false imaginations can come into our minds about a situation, and we may believe them. If we are not confident and not realistic about what we think of ourselves, or our ability to do things, we make decisions without even searching – or we may just "test" things out. So if there is a lack of faith, we can't proceed in life without it, because in our minds we are functioning in doubt and unbelief.

Sometimes we make excuses because we don't like something or someone, and it could be we have judged prematurely without even discovering who a person really is, or what is going on with the situation presented before us. We should give others the benefit of the doubt and an opportunity to display who they really are before we decide who we think they are. We should always be prayerful and not judgmental.

Jesus has told us that we must walk by the Spirit and not by our flesh; it is then that we can make the right decisions, and not out of our flesh. We must rely on the Holy Spirit, who is our helper and paraclete, the one who has been called alongside to help us when we need it – He's there to help!

Although this is not a spiritual statement, I would like to share an interesting and famous quote from Frank Ocean about what an excuse is. This may seem like a harsh statement, and it is not applicable to everyone, but it represents one person's view of excuses: "Excuses are the tools of the weak and incompetent. They build bridges to nowhere and tunnels to nothingness and those who excel in them seldom specialize in anything else."[4]

If we really break this statement down, the use of the word "weak" can be attributed to being weak in faith, and "incompetence" simply means not having the ability to complete something. The process here that does not seem to be complete is the effort and the time invested in dance technique. Granted, there may be a lot of reasons why something cannot be completed, but pertaining to this subject, there are always opportunities; it's just an issue of whether a person wants to take advantage of those opportunities. The second sentence tells us that we can't build, be equipped, or grow if we're not willing to learn; therefore, we're not building anything at all. If by chance an individual excels in their excuses, this is probably the best they will be able to build on, and not much else.

When we are being used as God's minister, we must always do a heart-check alignment. We should also make sure we are equipped to do what God has called us to do, especially if we are in a leadership role, and more importantly the fivefold ministry gifts because others are following us.

> *"And he gave the apostles, the prophets, the evangelists, the shepherds and teachers, to equip the saints for the work of ministry, for building up the body of Christ."*
> – Ephesians 4:11-12 (ESV)

In order to get to know the heart of the Father, we must know His Word and receive it in our hearts, and then we will be able to hear His voice. Although it may not be an audible voice, we can still be sensitive and in tune with the Holy Spirit, and we will be able to discern the difference. We should try to get to know the Lord more for our own selves as individuals, but it is especially important for those who are in leadership because people are following, and we need to lead by example. When our hearts are right before God, then our hearts are right before God's people.

Here is the order of knowing God's heart:

1. **Seek God** — to find or a desire to obtain or achieve. something. *"You will seek me and find me, when you seek me with all your heart."* – Jeremiah 29:13 (ESV)

2. **Listen** to His voice – give one's attention to a sound; the act of listening to something. *"When he has brought out all his own, he goes before them, and the sheep follow him, for they know his voice."* – John 10:4 (ESV)

3. **Discern** what God says – perceive or recognize something; distinguish with difficulty by sight or senses. *"My sheep hear my voice, and I know them, and they follow me."* – John 10:27 (ESV)[5]

When we come to God, we must come to Him with a pure heart and a contrite (humble) spirit (Psalm 51:17). As we cover ourselves with the water of the Word of God, and come to Him with thanksgiving in our hearts, then our hearts will be able to receive what He has to say to us. It will be as white as snow. Since we are His and He is ours, we must have open ears to hear what He has to say.

> *"Anyone with ears to hear should listen and understand!"*
> – Matthew 11:15 (NLT)

Let's take a moment and talk about David – King David! As we know, David made many mistakes in his decision-making, but God saw fit to speak to his heart. David's heart had a sinful nature, but his love for God had shown more. David is well known as a man who was after God's own heart, and because of this, David was extremely rewarded, slayed giants, and became king! Just as God's love towards David was great, His heart towards us is *so big*, and filled with so much love despite our shortcomings. He has so much to pour into our hearts, and when He does, we must be careful not to make decisions out of a sinful nature, but by the heart of the Father. Let's show how big our hearts are towards God.

The story of David shows us why it's so important that no matter what condition we are in, how we are living, and what we are saying, if we come to the Lord with a repentant heart and ask to receive His heart when making decisions, we will truly know what's in His heart and what He wants us to do. Listen to the voice of God, put your whole heart and trust in Him, and He will direct your decisions and your path. I know this may seem like a lot when talking about taking technique classes, but if we're going to use the statement "God knows my heart," then we want to make sure we know whose heart we are truly listening to. It is unbelievable that God would say, "I know your heart, my son/daughter, so you don't need to do that." Are we sure it's not our heart and our decision out of the flesh? Truly seek God about what He has to say about us taking time to improve our skill – the skill we use to serve Him.

Let's think about this: If God stood before us in human form, and we danced before Him, what would our moves look like, and would it be our very best? Have you utilized all resources to grow in your calling?

_____

_____

THE DANCE MINISTER AND DANCE TECHNIQUE

Are you as skilled in your dance as you are at your secular jobs, and is the effort to improve your gift from God worth making the investment in technique training?

_____

_____

It is not just God knowing our hearts, but also God seeing what we are doing to develop and invest in our worship towards Him. Our dance (movement) should be done in excellence by working to improve our gift. This would include knowing the Word, having an intimate relationship with Him, flowing in the Holy Spirit, always being prepared to move in the Spirit "literally" with our bodies, and incorporating training and techniques to better our gift just for Him.

LET US PRAY:

Father,

May we truly know Your heart. Let us truly know Your will and Your way for our lives – that our sinful hearts and nature turn towards You. As we minister to others, let it be Your heart that is reflected. Let it be the heart of You when we are making decisions, relating to others, and choosing to share Your heart through the ministry of dance. May we know whose heart we are sharing, and not let our flesh get in the way when making decisions about perfecting our gift of dance through technique. Let us be reminded that dance technique is a resource that You created for us, and we value every opportunity to grow. Oh, how excellent are Your ways! Make Your way our way, Your thoughts our thoughts, and may Your will be done in the earth through us as we carry Your heart within us.

In Jesus' name.

Amen.

CHAPTER 2

IT'S NOT ABOUT THE TECHNIQUE, IT'S ABOUT THE PASSION

Passion is such a strong and intense feeling. One will do almost anything and everything possible to get or accomplish something. There is hardly anything that will stop someone from doing what is necessary. Passion is so strong that it gives the feeling that nothing and no one can get in the way of it. It is rooted in love and can guide our emotions. The question is where our passion is derived from and in what way our passion is directed. Passion can take you down the path of righteousness, or it can take you down the path of deception. So it is important that we know what passion means, what passion is, and what we do with our passion.

The Merriam-Webster dictionary defines passion as "a strong feeling or emotion; great affection; and love." Passion is broken down into three categories:

- Love – Ardent affection; a strong liking or desire for or devotion to some activity, object, or concept; an object of desire or deep interest.

- Emotion – An intense, driving, or overmastering feeling or conviction. Emotions as distinguished from reason.
- Suffering – The state or capacity of being acted on by external agents or forces.[6]

How does our passion factor into God's passion? Our love for dance and our love for God must be parallel. The emotions that we feel when we dance should be driven by the same emotions that we have towards the Father.

Dancing for the Lord (by the Spirit) cannot be based solely on our passion alone because passion stems from our own personal feelings and emotions, and we should not be led and live by them "only"; we don't move in our passion only. Our passion does matter, and it is a part of who we are and what we love, but if we go before God's people and dance in our emotions and feelings (in our flesh), then we need to be very careful about that. This is why we should always present and consecrate ourselves before we minister and ask the Lord what He will have us do to minister to His people.

What is your version or understanding of passion as it pertains to the things of God?

_____
_____
_____

THE DANCE MINISTER AND DANCE TECHNIQUE

How does technique factor into your passion for dance?

_____

_____

_____

Let's talk in-depth about techniques to get a better understanding.

The Britannica Dictionary defines technique as "a way of doing something by using special knowledge or skill; the way that a person performs basic physical movements or skills."[7]

When we have a gift or talent and we train and practice, perfecting that craft, then we are utilizing the technique. Having a passion for dance goes hand in hand with dance technique training. We can have a love or strong feeling for dance that can build and grow by taking the movements to the next level, and by increasing our vocabulary and enhancing our movements. This is something some people do naturally (secular) – they go to dance school and take lessons, growing in skill and technique to eventually perform. When we dance for the Lord, we still have a passionate love, but we should also desire to take classes, *not to perform,* but to <u>minister</u> in dance effectively. Not only that, but there is so much more to learn about dance: its origin and history, and the vast dance vocabulary that explains the movements specifically.

Apostle Dr. Pamela Hardy is a renowned Christian leader, minister, teacher, author, prophet, and former professionally trained Broadway dancer/performer, who created and oversees the Eagles International

Training Institute in Texas and TEN Worldwide. She is a prime example of one who teaches and trains dancers from around the globe, not only teaching the biblical principles and foundations of dance but also incorporating dance techniques into the curriculum. From this well-rounded training, dance worshippers are licensed, equipped, and qualified to bring the gospel in dance throughout the world with boldness and confidence. The training encompasses the Word and technique. In her book *Dance: The Higher Call*, Dr. Hardy reminds us: "Technique makes a good gift better and skill makes a great gift excellent."[8] We can take our natural gift of dance and consistently combine it with technique to develop our dance language and abilities. Dr. Hardy often reminds us of the following scriptures:

> *"Do your best to present yourself to God as one approved, a worker who does not need to be ashamed and who correctly handles the word of truth."* – 2 Timothy 2:15 (NIV)
>
> *"Do you see someone skilled in their work? They will serve before kings; they will not serve before officials of low rank."* – Proverbs 22:29 (NIV)

What is your definition of technique, and how important is it to you and to God?

_____
_____
_____

Do you believe that taking technique classes takes away from your passion, and if so, why?

_____

_____

_____

Let's dive a bit into technique.

Technique training enhances our passion and the love we have for the Lord, and it does not mean taking a class is going to take away that passion. It's all about taking those moves rooted in your passion, ingrained with the movement of the Holy Spirit and utilizing technical skills to help you with your confidence, poise, grace, stamina, balance, and core strength. When we do this and develop our dance skills, God will be pleased, because we are taking the time to enhance our gift, become more skillful, and dance more in excellence for Him.

Being skilled means that we are equipped and capable of doing something well that we have taken the time to learn to do. The time that we've taken to learn is done through technique. Here are some examples of why it is important to be skilled:

- In Genesis 6:14, God called Noah to build the Ark before the Great Flood.

- In Exodus 26, God called women who were skilled in weaving to make the covers for the Tabernacle.

- When building Solomon's temple, Bezalel and Oholiab were called to transform the temple with their handiwork in Exodus 36.

Hopefully, these examples will further help us as dance ministers to understand the importance of skill and know that God's passion aligned with our passion will make the circle complete.

Oprah Winfrey has stated, "Follow your passion. It will lead you to your purpose."[9] Yes, our passion and what we are driven by will lead us to our purpose, but as Christians, followers of Christ, we must focus on the origin and root of our passion, so that we can truly determine our destiny and true purpose for us in God. We must check our hearts and evaluate our passion, spend time with the Lord, and hear who He wants us to be, what He wants us to do, and where He wants us to go. When we know this, we can set our goals and work towards them, and it will lead us to our purpose – God's purpose for our lives.

We cannot be led by our flesh feelings and driven by emotions, especially before we step on the altar. Remember, what's in us will come out, and if we are not spiritually in tune and covered in prayer before we minister, then all of those fleshly emotions and feelings that may have not been dealt with or presented before the Lord can potentially be conveyed before God's people: offense, depression, anger, bitterness, etc., making our dance just about our own passion. When we minister, it should be birthed out of prayer, which will produce a supernatural flow as opposed to a carnal flow.

We as worshippers – dancers, singers, musicians, mimes, painters, etc. – have been placed on the front line of battle before the men or women of God speak in our churches, and we set the tone and the atmosphere for the Holy Spirit to come into the room and move. We aid in mending broken hearts, healing bodies, and delivering from sin. When we are possibly put in a place of combat and war for the Kingdom, only the heart entwined with the passion of God will be the ammunition we need. How we are feeling in our flesh at that moment cannot take over, because the true passion from God, with the indwelling of the Holy Spirit, will matter and make a difference in the congregation's experience when we are ministering.

> *"Then Jehoshaphat consulted with the people and appointed those who would sing to the LORD and praise the splendor of His holiness. As they went out before the army, they were singing: "Give thanks to the LORD, for His loving devotion endures forever." The moment they began their shouts and praises, the LORD set ambushes against the men of Ammon, Moab, and Mount Seir who had come against Judah, and they were defeated." –* 2 Chronicles 20:21-22 (BSB)

For example, if we had an argument on the way to church or swore at someone before service, all of our personal emotions and feelings should cease the minute we hit the church house door. We must be in preparation mode for whatever comes. We will be dancing to what is on God's heart, and the love and passion we have for Him will be obvious – thus allowing us to be led by the Holy Spirit conveying God's message. God is expecting us, as His ministers, to be skilled and prepare ourselves for war. Our bodies must be strengthened, toned, and developed to be ready to complete the assignment God gives us, and we must be ready to dance it out at all costs! We must align our passion with what God is passionate about and be masterful and skillful in carrying it out.

We must be certain as dance ministers to discern which passion we are functioning in: our passion and desires, or God's passion, the passion of Christ. Is the passion we have the same as the Father? Did we seek Him about our passion, or do we spend more time making decisions regarding the things of God without truly consulting Him? When we have a true passion for the Lord, we want so much to learn from God, be a part of Him, and desire to know Him more. Out of this passion, we will yearn to grow in our faith and intimate relationship with Him, and as His dance ministers, this includes growing in skill. This shows that you treasure the gift He gave you, and that you will be and stay equipped to be called (suitable and adaptable) to minister when assigned, giving Him your very best.

When discussing taking a dance technique class, it is like we have said a bad word, and some do all they can to avoid talking about it, let alone taking it. Think about these questions:

1. Is it because it's new for you and you have already decided that you can't do it? Why do you feel that way?

_____

_____

_____

2. If you have some dance technique experience, do you think you have accomplished all there is to learn and do not need more training? Why is that?

_____

_____

_____

3. Is it because of the lack of money and resources?

_____

_____

_____

The big question is, are you not worth investing more into yourself, your talent, and your gift – your calling? Of course, you are! Is God worth us investing more time? Yes, indeed He is! Worshipping God in Spirit and in truth requires excellence and at times sacrificing for the Kingdom, and that means bettering your skill in dance! Let us not count ourselves out and think less of ourselves. We can do all things through Christ who strengthens us every day (Philippians 4:13). We must believe in ourselves.

LET US PRAY:

Heavenly Father,

I pray that we continue to be passionate after You – that our emotions line up with Your purpose for our lives. Let us make decisions not out of fleshly passion, but out of a passion led and guided by the Holy Spirit. As we continue to seek You, we are passionate for You and grateful for Your tender mercies; let Your will be done in our lives and let all those who witness our movements see the passion of Christ in us. Let our dance compel others to be passionate for You as well. Let us be passionate about dancing prophetically, as well as dance training, to enhance the gift You have so graciously given us. Help us to believe in ourselves, as You believe in us.

In Jesus' name.

Amen.

CHAPTER 3

DANCE SHOULD ONLY BE DONE SPONTANEOUSLY BY THE HOLY SPIRIT

Some dance ministers do not take dance technique training because they believe dancing for the Lord should be spontaneous *only*, completely unplanned, and there should be no dance training at all. This also excludes spending time creating choreography or teaching it to others to minister. "Spontaneous" means to do something based on impulse, or something that is not planned. When dancing spontaneously, one is simply compelled to move, and usually, it is when the music begins without listening to the entire song. However, dancing in the Spirit involves every aspect of the dance ministry experience.

Our dance is ministered unto the Lord, and no one way of worshipping God is more important than the other, whether it is spontaneous or choreographed. When dance is presented through prayer and study of the Word, the Holy Spirit is at work, assisting us in making our movements divinely inspired, whether we dance spontaneously or create choreography. Liturgical dance is when we as dance ministers dance, moving out the *liturgy* of the Word of God – a spiritual communion with the Lord, also known as "public worship."

By making the statement that dancing for the Lord should only be done by the Holy Spirit, are we saying the *only* way dance is inspired by the Holy Spirit is when it is spontaneous – meaning done without choreographing, rehearsing movement, or training? Can the Holy Spirit be involved in them all? Choreographed dance absolutely can and *does* involve the Holy Spirit. Invite Him in and He will be there. The Holy Spirit can inspire and empower your movements immediately or share them slowly and subtly – it can be imparted to us at any time.

> *"Jesus replied, 'It is not for you to know times or seasons that the Father has fixed by His own authority. But you will receive power when the Holy Spirit comes upon you, and you will be My witnesses in Jerusalem, and all Judea and Samaria, and to the ends of the earth.'"* – Acts 1:7-8 (BSB)

God has given us the Holy Spirit, who lives and dwells in us, and who leads and guides in all truth. When we pray in the Spirit, it enables the Holy Spirit to carry the message to the Father – it is an even exchange that is empowering. There is always a moving flow! As you know, when the Holy Spirit is flowing, He can influence our movements in whatever way they are presented – instantaneously, while creating movement over a period, or in a completed choreography that is taught to others. In God, we live, move, and have our being – literally!

> *"God intended that they would seek and perhaps reach out for Him and find Him, though He is not far from*

each one of us. For in Him we live and move and have our being." – Acts 17:27-28 (BSB)

One of the most important things we must keep in mind when we dance for the Lord is that everything, we do for God is derived from and starts with prayer. Prayer is our intimate time and conversation with the Father, where we receive direction, instruction, and even correction. When we spend time with the Lord in the following capacities, we are availing ourselves to Him to receive what He has for us:

1. The Holy Spirit can download movement to us spontaneously; it can happen on the spot, the moment the music comes on (not listening to the song beforehand).
2. The Holy Spirit can download our movements when we spend time listening to a worship song, and we can visually see the movements, create them, and move it out.
3. We can also receive a download of movements that we have created over time, and we may want to share with others, for them to do the same movements and eventually display them before God's people together.

When we put the supernatural (Holy Spirit) on the natural order of things, meaning taking what God created and imparts to us, we can teach the dance minister technically, and it is still inspired by the Holy Spirit. We must know all that has been created comes from God, by way of the Holy Spirit. Everything! Even in a dance technique class, the Holy Spirit is also present – He is everywhere.

If you believe movements of dance can only be inspired by the Holy Spirit spontaneously, then you are closing the door to other areas where the Holy Spirit can dwell also. God is not limited, and the Holy Spirit is not limited or placed in a box. He is a living, moving Spirit that can have His way in any arena, in any fashion, and at any time. There are dance ministers who will not accept the idea of taking time to create a dance or a choreography that is still spiritually inspired. They are denying themselves another opportunity to experience the Holy Spirit in a different way in their lives and in their ministries. Just because we've created something or planned something, that doesn't mean the Holy Spirit didn't give it to us. We depend on the Holy Spirit for so many things, and we cannot limit what the Holy Spirit can do.

There are also times when a dance minister will spend time listening to a song (usually for a brief period), and they can visualize movements, then get up and move out what they saw – unrehearsed. This is another form of a divine download. Just because you created the movement doesn't mean that God didn't give that to you. God is the Creator of the movement, and He can share with us His divine movements however He sees fit – at any place and at any time. We should never put a limit on what God can do. God is the Creator of heaven, earth, and all who inhabit the earth, and how wonderful that He has given us a gift to visually moves out the vision and we can be a blessing to those who watch and receive it. God created it, so He has given us the opportunity to create as well.

"In the beginning, God created the heavens and the earth. Now the earth was formless and empty, darkness

was over the surface of the deep, and the Spirit of God was hovering over the waters." – Genesis 1:1-2 (NIV)

"So God created mankind in his own image, in the image of God he created them; male and female he created them." – Genesis 1:27 (NIV)

From the scriptures, we can see that God is the Creator of life and all that dwells therein. He has given us the capacity to create dance movements, and it is not only for ourselves but also for those we see or encounter. The congregation comes to hear the Word, hear the songs, and in some churches witness the ministry of dance – praise and worship! By the way, worship is created and not always spontaneous, and so is the worship of dance. God can place a song on our heart, or the heart of our pastor, and we may be presented with an opportunity to either move instantaneously or move upon request for the future – by way of choreography – depending on the circumstances presented. When a presentation is requested at church for a specific occasion, it gives us an opportunity to share it with our dance ministry teams.

This is an example of a process that we can use when creating and preparing for a choreography:

- What is the occasion and the theme? It is important to know what we are ministering and why.
- What is the scripture that is related to the theme or the song that has been chosen?
- What is the song?

- Get the lyrics and listen to the song and let the words get into our hearts.

- Memorize the words.

- Pray, and ask the Lord to enlighten that scripture and give us a vision of how to move the words out – illuminate our minds and Spirit.

- Seek out the biblical colors that apply to the subject we are ministering about.

- Pray about what garments to wear.

- Provide this information to the team and begin to create choreography.

- Enter times of corporate prayer together to stay spiritually in tune with each other.

As you can see, God is involved in the process of all the steps mentioned. If a dance ministry team is not following spiritual protocol concerning their choreography, then the choreography is just a performance. Remember, God is a God of order, and He expects the gifts we use for praise and worship to be ministered to in an orderly and excellent fashion. Those who are in tune with the Holy Spirit will be able to discern if the choreography being ministered is anointed or not. It is important to maintain God's anointing by cleansing ourselves with the Word of God and renewing our minds.

"For you can all prophecy one by one, so that all may learn and all may be encouraged, and the spirits of

THE DANCE MINISTER AND DANCE TECHNIQUE

prophets are subject to prophets. For God is not a God of confusion but of peace." – 1 Corinthians 14:31-33 (ESV)

Being anointed means being empowered from on high – we carry God's Spirit, and we minister to encourage others and empower them to prosper in everything they do. The anointing should remove burdens (heaviness) and destroy the yokes (rope from around the neck) of bondage (no freedom); people should be healed and set free through our anointed movements.

We can dance technically and still be inspired by the Holy Spirit. Is the Holy Spirit limited by technique, or does adding technique deter us from the Holy Spirit? Absolutely not! Remember, dance technique is the process of taking care of your body and working on improving your movement. Learning dance techniques assists us with how to carry our bodies and how we center ourselves, which helps us with our rhythm and flow. Those who are committed to dancing for the Lord should be committed to perfecting the gift of dance that God has given us.

Do you believe you can dance technically and still be inspired by the Holy Spirit? Why or why not?

_____

_____

_____

The Holy Spirit can have His way in everything that we think, say, and do, and we can go into a dance technique class knowing that we have made God a part of our everyday lives by prayer and supplication. We can ask the Lord to give us the ability to learn and retain what is being taught and to help us as we practice. We can do it, and He is there to help; He will bring all things to our remembrance (John 14:26). All we have to do is ask.

Here are some reflections and testimonies from dance ministers who have experienced the Holy Spirit both spontaneously and choreographically:

> *"As I walked into the calling of dance for the Lord, I found myself lost and not knowing what direction to take. So many expectations and so many people were telling me what I was doing wrong. With all of this frustration, I walked into my church on the day of our first conference, and when I walked into the temple, I felt so much sadness and was ready to leave it all behind.*
>
> *I was going to minister a choreography that I had rehearsed and prepared for a long time, but something inside was missing. God had given me a song that was not very well known, and I wanted to dance to a song that everybody knew. As I was getting ready to start, a feeling of peace came over me, and I just heard "Let me do it." I was in love with the music, and I released my frustrations, anxieties, and pain. I felt my body release and the weight lift, and my soul and spirit were free. As I continued moving through the congregation, I realized that I was not at the front by the altar, but I was being guided to move around, and people were crying and on*

their knees. At that point, I knew the Holy Spirit was in control." – Minister Alicia Dapena-Pache - Revelation 12 Ministry, Salem, MA

We can clearly see that the Holy Spirit moved when this minister choreographed a ministry piece, and the Holy Spirit further intervened by prompting her to dance spontaneously (planned and unplanned), moving around the church. It ministered to both her and the congregation. Glory!

"I was asked to minister in dance at an event, and I prepared myself by praying, searching biblical foundations, and being led by the Holy Spirit, who then put the steps together.

As a result, everyone was laid out on the floor, and there was a heavy presence of the Holy Spirit in that place. People left rejoicing, sadness was lifted, and some were in shock and crying, but it was tears of joy that they expressed. Some women were healed, and some even said, "I'm going to dance with the Lord in my home." I heard another saying that God answered her prayer through the movement.

There was a time in my life when I didn't want to minister and dance anymore, but the Holy Spirit came in and restored me." – Pastor Johanna Diaz, Christlike Christian Church, Worcester, MA

We can see here how this dance minister took the necessary steps and sought the Lord on how to prepare to minister choreography to the people. Because the Holy Spirit was completely involved in that process, when she danced, chains were broken, bondages were released, and people were healed and set free. Not only were they free, but the dance minister was restored and received her breakthrough. Hallelujah!

LET US PRAY:

Father,

We are grateful that You are the author and finisher of our faith, and You know the beginning from the end. We count it an honor and a privilege to use the creativity You have given us for Your glory and as a blessing to others. As we dance for You, we know that when we have a relationship with You, You are orchestrating our movements, spontaneously and choreographically, by the Holy Spirit. We are grateful that You provide the vision, and we take it to heart and run with it. As we move for You, we thank You for the opportunity to grow technically, so that we can dance out the liturgy of the Word effectively with boldness and confidence.

In Jesus' name.

Amen

CHAPTER 4

I TRIED TAKING A TECHNIQUE CLASS AND I DON'T LIKE IT

Sometimes if we are trying out a dance technique class for the first time, we may feel uncomfortable because it's new to us. Some may become intimidated if there are students in the class who have more dance experience or pick up the technique quicker than others. Sometimes things in life do not come easy, but we must work at it and practice to be where we want to be. We also cannot compare ourselves to others because we all come from different backgrounds with different experiences. We are uniquely and wonderfully made by God. Just because one may be a beginner doesn't mean they cannot dance – everyone can dance! We all have our own rhythm, uniquely given to us by the Lord. We are God's perfect design, and we carry His rhythm!

> *"I will give thanks and praise to You, for I am fearfully and wonderfully made; Wonderful are Your works, And my soul knows it very well."* – Psalm 139:14 (AMP)

What about the dance class made you not like it? Was it because it was difficult, were you not able to grasp the timing or movements, or was it the genre of dance?

_____

_____

_____

We should try not to be afraid of new beginnings no matter how old we are, where we come from, or what level of dance we possess. Let us not forget, that we can do all things through Christ who strengthens us (Philippians 4:13). If taking technique classes is new to us, remember we must start somewhere – from the beginning. Even in the beginning of creation, there was a starting point where there was nothing (darkness, void), and God was able to create and move over the earth. He spoke His creations into existence, and so can we. Remember, it took God six days to finish the creation process, which tells us that things take time. With each day God created, there was a progression, and we will progress also.

"For God has not given us a spirit of timidity, but of power and love and discipline." – 2 Timothy 1:7 (NASB)

Just as God spoke and the world was manifested, we will have what we say – and so, what are we saying about the classes? We as Christians often confess that we can do all things when we know God is with us (Emanuel), but are we really walking that out and standing on that confession? We need to go into the class knowing that we are there to learn and that we eventually will get a hold of what is being taught. When we first gave our lives to the Lord, we were new to the understanding of who God was, and so we spent time getting to know Him. We read and reread the Word to really start grasping who God is, and we use different avenues to gain this knowledge: fasting, praying, studying, meditating, worshipping, praising, etc. It is the same for us as dance ministers: we use the avenues and resources available for us to be equipped, and part of that is technical training.

Please ask yourself, did I give the dance class a chance before giving up so quickly? If you did, why?

_____

_____

_____

Taking one or two classes will not fully show us what it can offer us, but taking more classes will open our eyes and expose us more to the beauty of the art of dance. Dance training is progressive, so we need to keep going and press through, and we will be surprised at what will happen! Having faith in God is awesome, but where is the faith in ourselves? In fact, where is our faith in God? We must have enough faith to believe that we will grow and flourish as we learn dance techniques, and know the Lord is with us. When we step out on faith, God will meet us there.

"Count it all joy, my brothers, when you meet trials of various kinds, for you know that the testing of your

faith produces steadfastness. And let steadfastness have its full effect, that you may be perfect and complete, lacking in nothing. If any of you lacks wisdom, let him ask God, who gives generously to all without reproach, and it will be given him. But let him ask in faith, with no doubting, for the one who doubts is like a wave of the sea that is driven and tossed by the wind." – James 1:2-6 (ESV)

If God asked us to do something that relates to our dance ministry call, would we do it if we didn't like the idea? We may say "Yes" to God and confess we will do what He wants us to do, be who He wants us to be, and go where He wants us to go – and if we say we have faith and want to please God, are we really saying "Hineni – Lord, here I am?"

Let us not only profess our Yes but also take steps towards what we have said. Remember, we say yes to God, no matter the cost. When it comes to enhancing our skills as dance ministers and pleasing God, we need to say yes to investing in our calling. How can we love to dance, but not want to know about its history, terminology, and genres? Dance is not exclusive, but vast and exciting with many genres. We must see the benefit of learning the basics of dance technique.

History has shown that some people do not like or want to take ballet specifically, which is the basics and foundation of dance. This expression has been shared by some who have not taken the class but have a preconceived notion about it, or by some who have taken one class and decided not to return without giving it a chance. We should not judge or make such a decision until we have fully engaged in the activity for a period and given ballet a chance. Speaking of judgment, it is human nature that we don't like to be judged (prejudged), but we want others to get to know us first before deciding who they think we are. Well, let's get to know the various genres of dance like ballet, modern dance, contemporary dance, lyrical, jazz, hip hop, African, tap, and more. There are so many forms of dance we can explore, where we can build our dance vocabulary, and our dance will speak more through our movement.

If the reason we don't take a dance technique class as dance ministers is due to finances, rather than not liking the class, then let's talk about it. If we want to take classes, then we can be creative in how we can work on that, and it first starts with the Lord. We must make it known to Him what we desire and have that mustard seed faith.

> *"Embrace this God-life. Really embrace it, and nothing will be too much for you. This mountain, for instance: Just say, 'Go jump in the lake' – no shuffling or hemming and hawing – and it's as good as done. That's why I urge you to pray for absolutely everything, ranging from small to large. Include everything as you embrace this God-life, and you'll get God's everything. And when you assume the posture of prayer, remember that it's not all asking."* – Mark 11:22-24 (MSG)

God can reveal different strategies and resources to us if we come to Him. We must pray, believe, and make our confession of faith. Here are some ideas:

If we have a service that can benefit the dance organization/studio, bartering has been a successful way to get free dance lessons. When we are bartering, we are providing a service that the organization can use, which could avail free classes or discounts on tuition:

1. Clean the rooms in the dance studio: floors, mirrors, ballet barre, bathroom, trash, etc.
2. Hold fundraisers for the organization. (Ideas – car wash, bake sale, etc.).
3. Help transport students to and from dance classes when parents are unable to.
4. Volunteer to drive traveling to/from competitions or be chaperones during the trips.
5. Help around the organization/studio: front desk coverage, collecting tuition payments, data entry, and billing.
6. Help with advertising the studio or marketing.
7. If you are a seamstress: help with alterations or make costumes/garments.
8. If you are a handy person: make repairs, paint, and fix things as needed.

Some of the ideas listed above can also assist with funding the following:

- Competition team fees, travel costs, and costumes.

- Costumes for recitals that students/parents may have trouble paying for.
- Funds towards recital costs: venue/site fee and tickets.

Another option to consider is having a technique teacher come to your location to teach, especially to teach the dance ministry team. If your dance ministry takes up periodic love offerings, or members pay dues, perhaps some of the funds can pay the technique teacher who comes on-site.

Let's discuss a few apprehensions or concerns we may have about taking dance technique classes. It is important to discuss them and be reassured that our concerns are addressed. Let's break barriers that have not allowed us to pursue taking dance technique classes.

Fear - This is the opposite of faith, and we must love and have faith in ourselves – think positive and know "we've got this." We are more than conquerors through Christ (Romans 8:37), and as long as God is with us, there is nothing we cannot overcome. Perhaps bringing a buddy/partner and taking classes together, or bringing a team, will not only relax your fears but also make it a great time of fellowship.

Finances - Try to be vigilant in budgeting and saving for dance lessons, and if it is taking time to get to where you need to be, be creative in how you can pay. As you strategize, seek out as many technique classes as possible: videos and social media provide many classes, and they are free!

Being judged - God is our judge and not man! What we do for God is what matters and what will last. He wants us to be at our very best as we function in our calling of dance, and there is training available to help us. Letting the Holy Spirit comfort us is the best ally we have against the enemy. Those who judge, talk about, or taunt us should not faze us, because God will be pleased, and we will build our confidence and soar!

Regardless of the reason or excuse we have given as to why we are not taking dance technique lessons, as we wait to hear from the Lord, we must know that He will make provision for us because He is *Jehovah Jireh* – our Provider. He is all we need, and His provision shall be seen in our lives! Continue to lift His name and thank Him in advance for what He is going to do. Just be still, believe, and know that God *is* God (Psalm 46:10).

> *"Therefore I tell you, do not worry about your life, what you will eat or drink; or about your body, what you will wear. Is not life more than food, and the body more than clothes? Look at the birds of the air; they do not sow or reap or store away in barns, and yet your heavenly Father feeds them. Are you not much more valuable than they? Can any one of you by worrying add a single hour to your life?"* – Matthew 6:25-27 (NIV)

LET US PRAY:

Dear Lord,

We thank You for giving us all things in life to enjoy. We are grateful for Your provision, and nothing is too hard for us, because we know that You are with us. Continue to instill in us all boldness and confidence in ourselves to know that we can do all things through You. Help us to clearly see the full picture and not assume things without gaining knowledge and understanding, as we earnestly pray for clarity. Let us not faint or be weary but embrace dance technique training as dance ministers and be consistent in the development process – never giving up or giving in. May Your provision continue to be seen in our lives as we dance for You.

In Jesus' name.

Amen.

CHAPTER 5

I DON'T NEED TECHNIQUE CLASSES

Some dance ministers do not think they need to take dance technique classes and believe these classes are not necessary. Taking dance classes can serve many purposes and it's more than just about the technique. We should first and foremost desire to maintain a healthy body because this is the body God has given us, and we have a responsibility to take care of it.

> *"I appeal to you, therefore, brothers, by the mercies of God, to present your bodies as a living sacrifice, holy and acceptable to God, which is your spiritual worship. Do not be conformed to this world, but be transformed by the renewal of your mind, that by testing you may discern what is the will of God, what is good and acceptable and perfect."* – Romans 12:1-2 (ESV)

As we dedicate our bodies to the Lord because we know we belong to Him, there are so many health benefits to dance training and exercise:

Healthline Magazine has an excellent article about the "8 Benefits of Dance":

1. **Dance improves cardiovascular health** — When we dance, our heart beats fast and assists in maintaining a good heart rate, which is about 60-100 beats per minute. It can improve our lungs for breathing as well.

2. **Improves balance and strength** — When we dance, we can improve our flexibility and stamina. It really builds up the center of our core. Our core is our stomach, back, hips, spine, pelvis, and bottom.

3. **Dance can be gentle on your body** — For those who are "gentle movers" or whose movements are limited, dances like ballroom dancing and line dancing are great forms of gentle dance movements.

4. **Boosts cognitive performance** — It was discovered that the area of our brain that controls memory and skills improve with exercise. Dancing can maintain and boost your ability to think as you age.

5. **Challenges your brain** — Dance is an excellent form of mental exercise for our minds. It requires us to focus on constant and changing movements as well as moves and patterns.

6. **Dance is all-inclusive** — Dance includes the entire body but can also include only certain portions of your body (e.g., upper-body or lower-body movements separately) All types are inclusive, and everyone can dance.

THE DANCE MINISTER AND DANCE TECHNIQUE

7. **Can be a social activity** – Dance is great for our social and emotional health. It is fun when we can dance and fellowship with others and just be around family and friends.

8. **Helps boost your mood** – Dance is a great stress reliever and helps with anxiety and stress. It can also boost self-esteem and allow us to be free and expressive. Dance releases endorphins that make one happy.[10]

When we as dance ministers are healthy, toned, and stretched, we not only will be able to do more when we move, especially when we are healthy, but it will get easier so that when we minister, we will spend less time on the technique and focus more on the ministry. The technique that we learn, and practice will become second nature to us as we minister; it becomes a part of who we are.

"Good technique will ensure a dancer's longevity, prevent injuries, build strength and flexibility, and refine movement quality. All of which provide technically skilled dancers with the ability to dance using correct body placement and alignment and beautiful lines…. Ultimately, it means moving efficiently." – Miss Robin Irey Marchiori, Cary-Grove Performing Arts Centre[11]

This statement pertains not only to technically trained dancers but also to those who have less dance training (including beginners). All dancers, regardless of experience, can train and learn more. We also should not let our age be a factor – we all can learn at any age.

Another thing to acknowledge is that dance is therapeutic. Dance allows us to be free, to express ourselves, and to release all that is bound up within us. So, the time we spend in class, training, learning to do different things with our bodies, and stretching out of our comfort zone into new levels is hard work, but great work. Dance training classes are excellent not only as a form of exercise for our health but also for our peace of mind and personal edification.

We should always be in a position of learning and being willing to learn so that we can teach others to serve more effectively and be more of what God wants us to be and what He wants us to do. Learning is an important mindset to have in our lives, including taking classes to perfect something that's related to our calling. It has been said that whether in ministry or in the secular world, we must be good students; we can never be great leaders and ministers if we are not willing to be students, even as we lead.

Do you think that as children of God, and as ministers of dance, we should be open to learning dance techniques? If so, what are your reasons?

_____
_____
_____

If not, please list your reasons why you do not think so.

_____
_____
_____

THE DANCE MINISTER AND DANCE TECHNIQUE

Taking a technique class will not take away from the ministry of dance; it is an asset. We truly need to be in a place where we are hearing from God about what to do and how to utilize our talent and gift of dance. As a reminder, the Holy Spirit imparts to us the movements, and all we are doing is equipping ourselves to enhance and perfect our gift and be an even greater blessing to the Body of Christ – and to the world.

> *"Whatever you have learned or received or heard from me, or seen in me – put it into practice. And the God of peace will be with you."* – Philippians 4:9 (NIV)

Some should truly think about why we are so against the technical training portion of being a dance minister. We need to be honest with ourselves and think about what God wants, and really come to terms with why we really don't think dance technique is necessary. Take it to God in prayer.

As a dancer, do you think being skilled would please God? Why or why not?

_____
_____
_____

If God asked you to do something that relates to your ministry, would you do it even if you didn't like the idea? Why or why not?

Dance ministers, whether technically trained or not, can minister. Adding dance technique is not going to take away from the natural talent of a dancer – with or without experience. It will not destroy the anointing, but becoming more skilled and diligent in our dance training will enhance the worship experience. God will truly be even more pleased! As an example, Joseph was diligent in his work in Potiphar's house, and after some time (processing time), he was advanced (promoted) and stood before Pharaoh. We can sit before royalty and find favor in the eyes of the Lord. God respects and will utilize our skills for His glory. We need to be committed to the process and prepared to be equipped and ready for our time of reward..

> *"Do you see a man who excels in his work? He will stand before kings; He will not stand before unknown men."*
> – Proverbs 22:29 (NKJV)

To reap the reward, we should make the sacrifice and put in the work towards more excellent worship. God honors our diligence and efforts, and if we take the time to get to the heart of the reasons why we think we don't need dance technique training, that will give us insight into when we should proceed with training.

Some may not recognize whether they are full of pride. We should consider if pride is the issue, make sure we know what pride is:

1. Pride will stop us from allowing other people to help us, because we may feel that we should do things all by ourselves. We could be embarrassed to tell people that we need help.
2. Pride is when you just think of yourself, and when it goes beyond that, a person can become arrogant or self-centered.

We must learn to be humble and know that we need the support of others. When we are humble, it's not going to stop us from allowing others to help us. A support system is something we should be able to trust, and we need to be open and vulnerable.

> *"Pride goes before destruction and a haughty spirit before a fall. It is better to be of a lowly spirit with the poor than to divide the spoil with the proud. Whoever gives thought to the word will discover good and be blessed is he who trusts in the Lord."* – Proverbs 16:18-20 (ESV)

Can you take a moment and evaluate if your decision of not needing to take dance technique training is a result of pride? If yes, will you reconsider and be open to pursuing it?

_____

_____

If not, why not?

_____

_____

Let us utilize the resources available to us and not allow pride or low self-esteem to make us closed-minded to things that can benefit and enhance our gift from the Lord and for the Lord. We should not let any circumstances, situations, people, or things, get in the way of elevating our purpose in God. We should try to be open-minded to the dance technique classes we initially think we do not like and give the dance lessons time. Let us not limit what God can do, or what He can do through us. Try to truly get the full training experience and watch God move!

LET US PRAY:

Heavenly Father,

As we continue to serve as Your ministers of dance, let us do all we can to enhance and perfect the talent and gift You have bestowed upon us. We ask that You create in us a meek and humble spirit (Psalm 51:10). Let us be reminded that to be skilled in our area of worship requires a commitment to technical dance training. We recognize that we may not want to commit to the process but let us remember that we need to and that if we do so, we will be taking steps forward to present before You our worship in a more excellent way. We want to make your heart happy and please You.

In Jesus' name.

Amen.

CHAPTER 6

I AM NOT TRYING TO BE A TECHNICAL DANCER

When a dance minister takes technique classes, it doesn't necessarily mean dance teachers are trying to "make us become technical dancers." They are there to help strengthen and stretch dancers to help them grow in their movement. Taking classes will never change who we are as a person, and no one can "make us" into someone or something else. We are made in the likeness and image of God, and we are who He has created us to be. God has placed situations, people, and things along our journey to assist us with what we are pursuing in life. If we decide we want to make a change about ourselves, learn something new, or enhance our gift, it is totally up to us. It is not always about someone else trying to change us against our will; it is about who we are, what our purpose is, and what we desire to do with the gifts God has given us.

In dance, it's about using our natural movements and possibly implementing training in technique to expand our dance knowledge and enhance our movement. Our natural movements and technical movements are joined together to make a perfect union. To reiterate, being skillful in dance will help us instill grace, maintain balance, build our core (our center), enhance our rhythm, and support and restore our confidence while we are dancing for the Lord.

We also must remember that dance is an art and a form of worship, and God is expecting us to have a process in place to maintain our dance, and to continue to worship Him in excellence. Dance technique is a worthwhile investment and can help propel our worship to the next level. Our bodies and how we use them are very important to God, and this includes various types of training. In working on our gift, including technical training, we must look at it as a process to better the gift and not try to force us to be something other than who God wants us to be.

Perhaps we should dig a little deeper into the definition of technique to be sure we have a true understanding of what it is and why it is important. Technique is defined as:

- The manner and ability with which an artist, writer, dancer, athlete, or the like employs the technical skills of a particular art or field of endeavor.
- The body of specialized procedures and methods used in any specific field, especially in an area of applied science.
- Method of performance; way of accomplishing.
- To apply procedures or methods to affect a desired result.[12]

Dance technique builds, forms, and places concentration on our body alignment. The structure and definition of our movements, especially as dance ministers, can be even more powerful, and the way we articulate them to the congregation can be life changing. The dance minister's body should be expected to move in such a way that hearts are filled, lives are transformed, spirits are uplifted, souls are edified, and new believers can be led to Christ.

Before technique comes into play, we briefly discussed that maintaining our spiritual health is first and foremost in our lives. We also know there is no one, and nothing, more important than the Lord, so while we are maintaining our spiritual health, we also must maintain our emotional, mental, and physical health. None of these areas should be excluded as we are building and growing.

We use a system in our everyday lives, building our spiritual technique, when we are studying the Word of God. We utilize these techniques, and it doesn't necessarily mean we are trying to become Bible scholars (although there's nothing wrong with being a Bible scholar). We usually study trying to get to the heart of the Father, to get to know Him more intimately, and to be in a relationship with Him. We may do some of the following to accomplish this:

- Read the Bible – Old and New Testament (There are 2,000 versions!).
- Research Hebrew and Greek words in Strong's Concordance.
- Devotions – professing and confessing the Word of God.
- Select a topic and study a particular subject.
- Meditate on specific scriptures and focus on them.
- Study the Word utilizing resources such as books, the internet, and videos.

It is unfortunate, but with some dance ministers, when taking a technique class is mentioned, it is almost like one is swearing or saying a bad word. There is nothing wrong with being a dance minister who is technically trained. There is also nothing wrong with a dance minister without training, but learning more about our talent/skill/calling is a benefit, so why do some make it sound sinful? It is as if technical training is being pinned against or put in competition with liturgical (sacred/praise/worship) dance when the two should go hand in hand; they work together. Both the more experienced and less experienced can learn a lot from each other and should coordinate efforts. The two are one.

> *"Behold, they are one people, and they have all one language, and this is only the beginning of what they will do. And nothing that they propose to do will now be impossible for them."* – Genesis 11:6 (ESV)

If doubting our capabilities or having low self-esteem is the reason for not wanting to take a dance technique class, as opposed to thinking that someone is trying to make us technical dancers, then it is worth exploring. It is great to have faith in God, but we must also have faith in ourselves. No matter what level we are at in dance, God values us where we are and can use us where we are. Every little step that is made towards heaven, through every movement, is a step closer to the Father. We cannot look to the right or the left to see if we are doing as well as someone else, because our movement and progress in dance is *our own*.

We need to truly believe in ourselves and keep going, no matter what the cost. At whatever level we are as dance ministers, we need to believe that we can do what we say that we can do. We say that life and death are in the power of the tongue, (Proverbs 18:21), but are we believing what we're saying? God has told us in His Word who we are, but do we really believe it? We say that faith is the substance of things hoped for, and the evidence of things that are unseen (Hebrews 11:1), and we may not see it now, but if we work towards it, we can get to where we want to be.

As a dance minister who has little or no technical training, what are you saying, and what do you really believe? Is your confession lining up with what you are doing to work on your calling? Share it below:

_____

_____

_____

It is unfortunate, but there are stories of less experienced dancers, or dancers with no technical training, who ministered in dance with all their heart and ability, and the congregation was receptive. This is wonderful because dance ministers need the confidence in knowing they are truly ministering to the congregation; however, we need to make sure the dance we display is led by the Spirit and anointed. There have also been times when the congregation does not appear to be as receptive as those with more technical skills minister in dance. It seemed as if the congregation didn't enjoy or receive the ministry provided by the more technically trained ministers. Was it because their movements seemed effortless compared to those with less training?

Does this mean dance ministers with more training are not anointed and the focus is only on technique? If yes, why do we think this?

_____

_____

_____

God is impartial and loves us all. He shows no favoritism towards a trained or untrained dancer. The anointing is the anointing, trained or not, and there are different levels of anointing. It is unfortunate that man has done this, and that we as dance ministers sometimes feed into it. This taints the heart of the dance minister, and this is when doubt and unbelief come; the desire to seek out dance technique training will not be a reality. We cannot let others determine where we go and what we do when it comes to our calling and what God wants us to do. That is between us and the Lord! We must act on His spoken word and not lend an ear to foolishness.

> *"Peter fairly exploded with his good news: 'It's God's own truth, nothing could be plainer: God plays no favorites! It makes no difference who you are or where you're from – if you want God and are ready to do as he says, the door is open. The Message he sent to the children of Israel – that through Jesus Christ everything is being put*

together again — well, he's doing it everywhere, among everyone.'" — Acts 10:34-36 (MSG)

A dance minister can portray what the movement means regardless of the experience, but experienced dancers should not be made to feel ashamed of their knowledge or experience, or to downplay their movements to accommodate the feelings of those with less experience. Likewise, those with less dance training cannot be made to feel that they are less than who God has called them to be, and they should never compare themselves. Dancers with no experience, a little experience, or much experience all have a purpose and a place in God, and no one should feel less than. When ministering, we cannot allow things like that to quench the movement of the Holy Spirit. There should be no measurement of worship, and many forget that dance is a form of worship art. Dance ministers, as well as the congregation, need to know that ministering in dance is not a performance and there is no competition; one's dance ministry level should never be compared to another, ever.

"As iron sharpens iron, so one person sharpens another. The one who guards a fig tree will eat its fruit, and whoever protects their master will be honored. As water reflects the face, so one's life reflects the heart." — Proverbs 27:17-19 (NIV)

As dance ministers, we need to be confident in who God has called us to be. We must believe in ourselves, even though we have not seen it yet. We need to take God at His Word and know that His Word is true concerning us. We cannot allow anyone to sway our decisions or negatively influence us. If we know that we have a talent and a gift from God, there is nothing wrong with learning more about it and bettering what we're doing. We live this life every day, and we learn something every day. How much more can we learn about this gift that God has given us as dance ministers? We should always be able to grow and expand our knowledge of dance. The opportunities are there to take advantage of, and it does not necessarily mean that someone is trying to make you into something else. Just look at technical training as an enhancement opportunity – another level in God.

LET US PRAY:

Father God,

We thank You for making us in Your likeness and image. As we strive to be the best that we can be, we are grateful that You have chosen us and given us this great assignment to be ministers of dance. As we lean on the guidance of the Holy Spirit, we will dance prophetically, releasing Your anointing into the atmosphere. Adding technical dance training will not change us into someone else but will only elevate our dance to another level. As we grow in our calling to minister in dance, we count it an honor and a privilege to serve. We are confident in our assignment, and we know who we are and whose we are.

In Jesus' name.

Amen.

CHAPTER 7

THERE ARE NO (ADULT) CLASSES IN MY AREA

Today, when we want to do something in life, there are so many resources and avenues when we seek them out. When it comes to taking dance technique classes, we have more options than we may have had some years ago. Taking a dance class is much more available to us today, even as adults. There are those who are truly seeking out these classes, and then there are those who are not. If we really want something, we will work hard to find it, and if we can't find it, there are people and other resources available to us. To start the search process, we must ask ourselves if we are really interested in taking dance technique training as dance ministers. If we are, the Word of God tells us that if we seek, we shall find (Matthew 7:7).

God has many scriptures regarding seeking because whenever God's presence was not with people, He would make sure to remind them about seeking Him. God wants us to seek His presence continuously. Since we are His ministers of dance, we should be seeking more opportunities to learn about Him, as well as about the gift of dance.

"Then you will call upon me and come and pray to me, and I will hear you. You will seek me and find me when you seek me with all your heart. I will be found by you, declares the Lord, and I will restore your fortunes and gather you from all the nations and all the places where I have driven you, declares the Lord." – Jeremiah 29:12-14 (ESV)

"For everyone who asks receives, and the one who seeks finds, and to the one who knocks it will be opened" – Matthew 7:8 (ESV)

When we are seeking something, we are pursuing and following it to the fullest. When we seek, we take time to explore and pursue the things we desire. Just think about how much we desire the presence of God and how the Spirit of God draws us closer to Him. We should be just as adamant about the desire to learn technique, and then continue this training so that we can not only be skilled, and minister more effectively but also pass what we have learned on to others.

Let's dive more into what seeking means. According to Dictionary.com, "to seek" is defined as:

1. To go in search or quest of; to seek the truth.
2. To try to find or discover by searching or questioning.
3. To try to obtain.
4. To go to.[13]

Seeking is searching. When we are seeking, that means we are searching for answers – in pursuit – and when we are in pursuit, we are looking to understand. If we in our own strength cannot comprehend or understand the answer or do not know it, that is when most would enter prayer and ask the Holy Spirit to search our hearts and reveal to us the answer. This is the one way for us to make decisions in our lives, *but* the order should be reversed. When presented with deciding we should go to God first and not try to do things in our own flesh by making decisions without Him in the beginning.

When we came into the true knowledge of God, and when He revealed to us our calling in dance, did we spend time and seek out the goals, plans, and steps towards the implementation of our calling? Did we write the vision and list said goals, plans, and steps, then act towards what was written? God has told us to write the vision and make it plain (Habakkuk 2:2), and part of the vision is doing research (seeking) to help accomplish our goals, seeking resources and people who can help to expand our knowledge and help educate us along the way.

How much time and effort have you invested in seeking out places to learn more about dance technique? If you haven't, why not?

_____

_____

_____

During our research, we may find that dance classes are predominantly available for children, and *maybe* some studios have adult classes. Although children have been the dominant audience for dance classes, there are more adult classes than ever before. If, for any reason, a dance minister lives in a location where there are no dance classes for adults, there are other ways of finding and participating in dance technique classes. Here are some resources that can help with our pursuit of growing technically in dance:

A. In-person group or private dance classes:

We can go online and search for a dance school in our area, either by name or zip code. We can't be afraid to venture outside of our local and surrounding community to attend a dance school if it's relatively close. They say anything worthwhile is worth the drive. While searching for an in-person adult class, you can request private lessons as an option, or get a group of people and approach the dance school to negotiate lessons at a mutually agreed time.

B. Dance CDs/DVDs and online videos:

There are many CDs/DVDs online for purchase. You can look them up on search engines like Google by genres of dance (ballet, jazz, contemporary, lyrical, tap, African, etc.), or by dance companies/schools or choreographers. You can also go on the internet and look on search engines for sites like YouTube and watch videos for free as opposed to purchasing them. Dance teams can also get together either at church or in each other's homes and follow the classes on DVD together.

C. Online group or private dance classes:

If you check social media (Facebook, Instagram. etc.), you will find advertisements from individuals who offer virtual groups or private dance classes on platforms like Zoom videoconferencing. There are ways to take a dance technique class online with a group of people where they can see the teacher, and the teacher can see them, but the students cannot see each other. It would still be like taking a private class. *(I personally teach group and private dance classes on Zoom videoconferencing, and it is a great alternative for dancers to learn from home.)*

D. Schedule a dance teacher to teach on-site:

Another opportunity to take dance technique classes is to invite a dance technique teacher to your location or to hold a dance ministry meeting/rehearsal on a regular or periodic basis where the teacher can come and teach on-site. This is a great way to cut back on expenses by sharing the expenses with the team/group. *(I have a portable ballet barre, and when requested, I go on-site and teach technique classes.)*

E. Dance technique teacher within the group/team:

Another thing to consider is that within some dance ministry teams, we can take advantage of being taught on-site by a technique dancer/teacher who is a part of the dance ministry team. If dance techniques are incorporated into our dance ministries as part of the curriculum, we can solve the challenge of having to look for a dance studio. Either that person can do it for free as part of the ministry curriculum, or the team can take up a love offering and be a blessing.

If we take time and try to pursue dance technique training through one of the resources listed above, it can help us to develop our skills, give us an opportunity to collaborate with each other, and build our communication and relationship with each other in a wonderful way. It will also help develop our God-given creativity.

LET US PRAY:

Lord,

We are thankful that You are Jehovah Jireh, and Your provision shall be seen in our lives. You always make a way out of no way, and You will see us through as we search for dance technique training classes. As we venture and research to find the people, places, and things that will assist us in our dance training pursuit, we believe that You will provide the resources that we are looking for, from the North, South, East, and West. We are grateful for the people and opportunities that You will put in our path as we travel this journey with You.

In Jesus' name.

Amen.

CHAPTER 8

I DON'T WANT TO LEARN FROM 'XYZ'

In our pursuit of educating ourselves as dance ministers in dance technique, it is important to select classes that offer ballet basics, as well as other genres of dance. Since ballet is a dancer's core study of the art of dance, it is also important to be selective in who we choose to teach us. Unfortunately, some dance ministers have been heard saying they do not want to learn from certain teachers, based on some of the following reasons (excuses?). We will use "XYZ" as an anonymous name in each example:

- "I don't know XYZ and have never heard of him/her."
- "XYZ is not a friend of mine, so I am not comfortable taking his/her class."
- "XYZ doesn't look like they dance well, and they probably cannot teach well either."
- "XYZ is friends with someone I do not like."
- "My friends told me some things about XYZ, and I am not interested in learning from him/her."

- "I know XYZ from (church, our dance ministry, work, etc.), so I would rather learn from someone else."
- "I have already taken a class with XYZ, and he/she taught the same thing in another class I took."
- "XYZ is not a well-known teacher globally, and I would rather learn from someone who is well-known globally."
- "XYZ is not a Christian, and I don't want to learn from them."

Have you said or thought about any of these reasons and based your decisions on them? Have you ever considered why you think or thought this way? Why?

_____

_____

_____

Yes, we should have set criteria when selecting whom we learn from, but we should not judge people before knowing who they are, researching information about them, or finding credible references. If none of these are sufficient, we should at least consider giving individuals a chance before prejudging; we may just be wrong about what we think or perceive.

What does it mean to judge someone? When we judge someone, we have thoughts that are predetermined, and at times, it happens before we get to know a person. There are also scenarios where we hear about a person and make an instant decision about who they are before getting to know them. When we take the time necessary to research, we will be able to form a constructive and objective decision – and this type of judgment is very different.

Let's look at what God says about judgment:

> *"Don't judge, so that you won't be judged. For with whatever judgment you judge, you will be judged; and with whatever measure you measure, it will be measured to you. Why do you see the speck that is in your brother's eye, but don't consider the beam that is in your own eye?"* – Matthew 7:1-3 (WEB)

God doesn't want us to judge others based on their faults, imperfections, or sins. In His Word, it says we can judge, but based on one's actions – those that we see for ourselves, not based on what another person says. If we condemn others, we will be condemned as well. God is the one who searches our hearts and knows our thoughts and our intentions. We must recognize that only He is the ultimate judge.

Let's look over our list again and address each reason/excuse:

- "I don't know XYZ and have never heard of him/her."

When we do not have information about a particular dance technique teacher, this is a perfect opportunity to use resources like the internet or even word of mouth, but we may also need to take into consideration that people will have their own opinions, which potentially may not be positive. You can take in some of that information but continue to research on your own to form your own opinion. Getting references from those who have taken classes is another alternative. If this person has a good reputation and following, it may be worth checking out.

- "XYZ is not a friend of mine, so I am not comfortable taking his/her class."

It shouldn't always matter who teaches dance technique – it can be either a friend or someone you do not know. Just keep in mind that in either situation, the focus is learning the technique necessary to improve your dance. Sometimes, it may be a good idea to branch out and meet new people. We should be open to learning from people we do not know, as well as those we do know. It's good to be objective when making decisions and checking references. God is not a respecter of persons (Romans 2:11), and neither should we be.

- "XYZ doesn't look like they dance well, and they probably cannot teach well either."

Just as beauty is in the eye of the beholder, so is one's dance. We all have opinions about what we see, and a person's dance presentation may not look pleasing to us, but that does not necessarily mean he/she is not a good dance technique teacher. Some dancers are better teachers, and some teachers are better dancers. There are even dance teachers who no longer dance themselves and only teach, which can be done. The only way we will ever find out is to try a class and see for ourselves. Pray about it.

- "XYZ is friends with someone I do not like."

In life, there are going to be people we don't like (or think we don't like) who have some sort of relationship with our friends. We need to realize that our friends have their own relationships, and that should not infringe on the choices we make. We must learn to separate the issue and focus on what is going to benefit our purpose and calling. We should also examine our hearts concerning why we really dislike the person, if what we feel is valid, and why we feel that way. We should take this situation to the Lord in prayer.

- "My friends told me some things about XYZ, and I am not interested in learning from him/her."

We should never be speaking against anyone and being a part of gossip. If we even lend an ear to it, then we *are* gossipers. It is only when we have discovered for ourselves that it is not beneficial to learn from a particular person that we should not take that person's class. We should not form an opinion based on someone else's encounter or experience without getting to know people for ourselves. Remember, God tells us to believe in the best of every person (1 Corinthians 13:7).

- "I know XYZ from (church, school, work, etc.), so I would rather learn from someone else."

It is understandable that sometimes we need to separate one area of our lives from another, but we should still be open to the possibility that someone from one of those areas may possess the skill we can learn from. We may think we know someone, but they may have skills and qualifications we may not know of. We can ask the Holy Spirit to reveal to us what is best and who is best for us.

- "I have already taken a class with XYZ, and he/she taught the same thing in another class I took."

Sometimes when we explore and take a ballet class, for instance, and we go back for another class and see that some of the same things are being taught, that is because basic ballet technique and terminology are taught repetitively for both beginners and professionals. As we continue to take dance classes, we learn additional terminology and technique. We should be faithful in pursuing classes further so that we can learn more and build our dance vocabulary and skill. God honors our faithfulness and obedience.

- "XYZ is not a well-known teacher globally, and I would rather learn from someone who is well-known globally."

It is awesome to learn from dance technique teachers who are globally known, but we can also learn from teachers who are in our local and surrounding areas. Those who are successful globally most likely started their dance training locally or regionally before they became who they are today. What is most important is to learn dance technique, and we can learn and grow in dance from those who teach both locally and globally. There are many qualified teachers and a variety of dance genres to choose from, and we can learn from so many places – near and far. God has given us so much to choose from and so many skilled and anointed teachers.

- "XYZ is not a Christian, and I don't want to learn from them."

The most optimal way of learning dance technique is from a Christian dance technique teacher. However, if there is not one available near us, there is nothing wrong with utilizing a dance technique teacher who is not a Christian. Most dancers start out at secular dance studios, and it is the technique that we're learning. From there, we can take what we've learned and implement those skills in our dance for the Lord.

> *"Love bears up under anything and everything that comes, is ever ready to believe the best of every person, its hopes are fadeless under all circumstances, and it endures everything [without weakening]. Love never fails [never fades out or becomes obsolete or comes to an end]. As for prophecy [the gift of interpreting the divine will and purpose], it will be fulfilled and pass away; as for tongues, they will be destroyed and cease; as for knowledge, it will pass away [it will lose its value and be superseded by truth]."* – 1 Corinthians 13:7-8 (AMPC)

God has let us know in His Word how important our love walk should be and how our decisions are affected without it. If we were to practice what we learn from the Lord, we may not have the mindset that we do sometimes concerning people mentioned on the list above. We are ministering to people and trying to win their hearts for Jesus so that they will give their lives to Him. We can't be one way when we're trying to minister, and then act another way outside of ministry. The way we are during ministry should align with how we are in our everyday lives. We should have the same mindset. Remember, love conquers all, and having the right heart, the right mind, and the right spirit when dealing with each other holds value and promotes respect.

THE DANCE MINISTER AND DANCE TECHNIQUE

Have you experienced any of the situations on the list? How did you handle it?

_____

_____

_____

LET US PRAY:

Dear Lord.

As You make us instruments of Your peace, please let us be reminded to love at all times. Help us to believe in the best of every person and to get to know our brothers and sisters in Christ. Let us not judge others negatively but keep our hearts and minds open to learning from those we may not know. Let us look at each other as You look at us, O God, and not single people out or show judgment against them. May we place a value on their gifts and give them a chance like You have given us many times. Let us remember that love conquers all, and may we have Your agape love and love unconditionally.

In Jesus' name.

Amen.

CHAPTER 9

WAITING TO GO ONLY TO THE CONFERENCE/WORKSHOP XYZ IS TEACHING AT

There are many dance ministry workshops and conferences scheduled throughout the year, nationwide and globally. It is highly recommended to attend them as much as one possibly can. Attending conferences and workshops is another way to gain more information about worship in dance and the biblical foundations, as well as to receive dance technique training. There are many anointed and well-known dance ministry leaders and dance ministers that we can learn from. It is definitely a worthwhile investment.

For those who are not certain of the difference between a workshop and a conference, let us define what they are and how they benefit us as dancers and ministers:

A. **Workshops** – Workshops are generally small or short events that may be for one day, part of a day, or multiple short days, and are usually directed towards educational training. Usually, workshops are more hands-on or intimate, involving specific topics of discussion, activities, or exercises. A workshop is heavily concentrated on a specific theme or subject. If we are looking for specific, more intimate, and focused training, then a workshop may be what we are looking for.

B. **Conferences** – Conferences are usually larger events that involve multiple speakers and various presenters, and sometimes vendors. Some conferences last multiple days as well. It is an opportunity to learn from a group of presenters and teachers, with a breakdown of sessions on specific subjects related to the theme of the conference. If we are looking for an event concentrating on multiple topics and discussions, then a conference may be what we are looking for.

Please note: Some conferences are so large that they can include workshops within their program or agenda, to offer an even more focused training in certain subjects or topics.

It would be beneficial for dance ministers to research biblical teachers and speakers, as well as technique teachers, and to connect with other dance ministers to gain information and obtain references. Once we seek out and find reputable and anointed instructors, we need to ask ourselves if we are open and willing to learn from them, even if we have never learned from them before. We should also consider not limiting our attendance at conferences and workshops to only once a year because there is so much, we can learn, and so many people we can learn from.

Participating in large, broad events like conferences and workshops is a great opportunity not only to learn but also to meet other like-minded Christians and dancers and to fellowship with them. There is so much we can learn from each other and so many experiences we can share.

> *"As iron sharpens iron, so one person sharpens another."*
> – Proverbs 27:17 (NIV)

> *"For the word of God is living and active, sharper than any two-edged sword, piercing to the division of soul and of spirit, of joints and of marrow, and discerning the thoughts and intentions of the heart."* – Hebrews 4:12 (ESV)

How important is attending dance ministry workshops and conferences to you? Why, or why not?

_____

_____

_____

Are you open to attending events with ministers and teachers you do not know? Why or why not?

_____

_____

_____

As ministers of dance, we should think about the types of workshops and conferences we want to learn from. We can determine what exactly we want to learn about, as well as who we want to learn from. While we are making plans to attend specific workshops and conferences, we may consider evaluating the following:

1. Where are we ministry-wise, and what is it that we're interested in learning about biblically?
2. As dancers, where are we technically, and how much more do we want to learn?
3. What genre of dance are we interested in?
4. Who will be speaking and teaching?
5. What are the finances involved?
6. What resources can assist us in attending?
7. Do we know anyone or a group of people attending the event that we can share expenses with?
8. If no one is going with you, you could contact the conference and decide on a roommate. Are you comfortable doing that?

Now that we have done our research and checked our resources when choosing a workshop/conference, we should not limit ourselves to just one particular event because Teacher XYZ is teaching there. I am not saying *not* to attend that teacher's event, because if we are receiving what we need from Teacher XYZ, we should continue to attend their conferences and workshops – as long as the biblical foundation and technique training are assisting in our growth, However, some dance ministers will not attend events taught by any other teachers or speakers, only Teacher XYZ. By doing this, we limit opportunities to be exposed to more. We may be able to add more to what we are learning, as there are so many different views, styles, and types of teaching we can learn. Getting a variety of information and training is great because we are expanding our knowledge beyond what is familiar.

THE DANCE MINISTER AND DANCE TECHNIQUE

"Do not neglect the gift you have, which was given to you by prophecy when the council of elders laid their hands on you. Practice these things, and immerse yourself in them, so that all may see your progress. Keep a close watch on yourself and on the teaching. Persist in this, for by so doing you will save both yourself and your hearers." – 1 Timothy 4:14-16 (ESV)

As always, God asks us to use wisdom, and wisdom says for us to do our due diligence by researching the leaders and teachers, as well as by seeking out references from those who may have attended those particular conferences and workshops. God has told us in His Word to explore new paths, resources, and ways of learning; He will do what is necessary to transform us into who He wants us to be, and He will direct our path. Whatever God has spoken to us and whatever He has promised, He will bring it to fruition.

As we take part in the learning process of attending workshops/conferences, it gives us as dance ministers an opportunity to take what we have learned and bring it back to our dance ministries to teach them. If there is a possibility for the dance team to attend the events, it is a great time of fellowship, worship, and bonding with each other.

LET US PRAY:

Heavenly Father,

As we pursue improving the gift of dance that You have given us, let us not limit whom we learn from. We recognize, God, that You have appointed and anointed many ministers in the body of Christ who can be a blessing in our lives. As we continue to support those ministers and teachers who have poured into us, let us also search for other dance ministries and technical dance workshops and conferences to attend. We will yield to the leading of the Holy Spirit, who will lead us to where and from whom we need to learn.

In Jesus' name.

Amen.

CHAPTER #10

XYZ IS A DANCE TEACHER IN OUR MINISTRY, BUT WE DON'T USE HIM/HER

When dance leaders are appointed and given the assignment of leadership, we are given the awesome responsibility to lead, edify, and exhort a team or group of people of all ages and backgrounds in ministry. What we teach and how we influence others is an awesome responsibility of servanthood. Let us look at how powerful and strong leading, exhorting, and edifying is:

Lead – to provide guidance or direction, having influence over others to get tasks or projects accomplished. We take a part in the direction of where others will go, and God is counting on us to lead and guide with authority, yet with a heart of compassion. (Strong's Hebrew Concordance 5148: "nachah" – to lead, guide.)

"Pay careful attention to yourselves and to all the flock, in which the Holy Spirit has made you overseers, to care for the church of God, which he obtained with his own blood." – Acts 20:28 (ESV)

Leaders serve in a shepherd-like role, leading their flock (team/members), and in turn, the sheep will follow. So, the influence of the dance leader can be either beneficial or detrimental to the growth of each member of the team. Also, the decisions that we make as leaders need to be in the best interest of our team first, and not of ourselves only. Leadership is based on what's best for the entire team.

Exhort – To strongly encourage or persuade someone or something to be done. To fill up with encouragement – cheer and support. (Strong's Hebrew Concordance 5749: "uwd" – to admonish, charge.)

"Let the word of Christ dwell in you richly, teaching and admonishing one another in all wisdom, singing psalms and hymns and spiritual songs, with thankfulness in your hearts to God. And whatever you do, in word or deed, do everything in the name of the Lord Jesus, giving thanks to God the Father through him." – Colossians 3:16-17 (ESV)

Leaders place such a significant role on the growth of the dance ministry team, and outside of the role of the senior pastors, we are under his/her authority as close as one can get. As leaders, we are to lead others into all truth, leading by example – God's example. We are His representatives on the earth, and it is important that we are objective and impartial when dealing with and working with our dance ministry teams. We need to be their cheerleader and at the same time charge them to explore God and go beyond what they know – elevate them!

Edify – to help, build up, and encourage others, as well as to educate and instruct. It also means to coach, train, and equip. (Strong's Hebrew Concordance 5790: "uth"- to help.)

> *"To equip his people for works of service, so that the body of Christ may be built up until we all reach unity in the faith and in the knowledge of the Son of God and become mature, attaining to the whole measure of the fullness of Christ."* – Ephesians 4:12-13 (NIV)

We as leaders should make sure that we are prepared and equipped to teach and to equip others. We should make every effort to find tools to educate and provide training to help edify our teams, so that they can explore opportunities and grow as dance ministers in biblical foundation, worship, dancing in the prophetic, and dance technical training.

Is technique an intricate part of your dance ministry curriculum or dance rehearsals? Why or why not?

_____

_____

_____

To have an effective and anointed dance ministry team that is functioning of one accord, we should value and utilize all the gifts that each member has. Utilizing the gifts of our teams should never usurp the authority of a dance ministry leader – in fact, it will enhance the relationship between the leaders and members and contribute to the growth of the dance ministry as a whole.

There may be members of the dance team who have talents and skills that dance leaders do not have, or members may have more experience in certain areas than the dance leader. We should earnestly utilize everyone's best gifts in some capacity. To add value to others, we need to value them and their gifts.

> *"Forget about deciding what's right for each other. Here's what you need to be concerned about: that you don't get in the way of someone else, making life more difficult than it already is. I'm convinced – Jesus convinced me! – that everything as it is in itself is holy. We, of course, by the way we treat it or talk about it, can contaminate it."* – Romans 14:13-14 (MSG)

There are some dance leaders who will not utilize the strengths and skills of some of their team members, because a team member may give the impression that they are trying to lead or usurp the leader's authority. Whatever it is – for example, biblical knowledge, prophecy, or dance technique skills – it should be looked at as a contributing factor. Sometimes it may *appear* that a member is trying to "take over" and it just may not be the case, and a leader should never allow themselves to feel intimidated or insecure.

If this is indeed the issue, it should be addressed for clarity and understanding, because good communication is key to avoiding any misunderstandings. When we have our ministry Bible studies and dance rehearsals that include times of prayer, fasting, and fellowship, it will give us time to truly get to know each other, both in the natural and by the Spirit, thus reducing the appearance of what may be perceived as evil or going against authority.

> *"Love bears all things [regardless of what comes], believes all things [looking for the best in each one], hopes all things [remaining steadfast during difficult times], endures all things [without weakening]."* – 1 Corinthians 13:7 (AMP)

Unfortunately, there are also times when certain leaders will not utilize the skills and gifts of some of their team members, because they may be viewed as "just" Sister XYZ or Brother XYZ. Just because we may have served with people we have known for years, and think we know everything there is to know about that person, that doesn't mean they should be disqualified from having their skills utilized on the team. They are not "just" anyone, and we don't always know what there is to know – let us not assume or take anyone for granted. That is called a spirit of familiarity.

> *"The spirit of familiarity is a spirit that causes people who are close to someone to become lax and depreciative of a connection or relationship with someone. It often comes into play with people who are close to those around them who have great anointing. People may be close to*

their Pastor or mentor so much so that they see their flaws." – Rev. Francis Obed Fornah, G.R.A.C.E. Ministries International, Inc.

Is Sister/Brother XYZ "just" XYZ because you may think you know that person? Can you see beyond what is familiar?

_____

_____

_____

Are you looking at what you think of Sister/Brother XYZ, or how their skill can be a blessing to the dance ministry team? What are your reasons for not learning from Sister or Brother XYZ?

_____

_____

_____

In Mark 6, we see that Jesus went to His hometown of Nazareth and people knew of His great teachings, mighty works, and healings. When He preached His sermon on the Sabbath in the synagogue, the people became too familiar with Him, believing in their own doctrines, and would not receive Him. Jesus was with His own people and was not accepted. So, Jesus had to go elsewhere to minister – we are talking about Jesus here!

He must have been surprised and even hurt by the rejection, but He was about His Father's business and had to dust off His feet and leave His own home. If a team member is overlooked, their gift or skill is not accepted, or they feel rejected, we should re-evaluate the relationship and not allow our flesh or judgment to drive away our team members. We need to remember this scripture:

> *"I am the vine; you are the branches. If you remain in me and I in you, you will bear much fruit; apart from me you can do nothing. If you do not remain in me, you are like a branch that is thrown away and withers; such branches are picked up, thrown into the fire and burned. If you remain in me and my words remain in you, ask whatever you wish, and it will be done for you. This is to my Father's glory, that you bear much fruit, showing yourselves to be my disciples."* – John 15:5-8 (NIV)

Is the reason you will not utilize the skills of Sister/Brother XYZ because they have more skills than you? What are the reasons?

_____

_____

Is a technique teacher in your ministry being utilized? If not, why not?

_____

_____

We do not want any of our team members to feel rejected or not valued. Let us not lose the anointing over a spirit of familiarity. Let us not have our blessings blocked, either as an individual or as a dance ministry (church), because of something that can be prevented. It is unfortunate that some dance ministries will seek outside of their ministries and churches for teachers and speakers to minister rather than utilize some of the gifts that are sitting right in their midst. Let us try to see others as God sees them and consider utilizing the skills of others on the team that will contribute to the equipping and edification of the dance ministry team.

LET US PRAY:

Father God,

As dance ministers and leaders, let us treasure the gifts of others in our sphere of influence or team. Let us consider utilizing the gifts of those among us, which can benefit and be a blessing as we seek out dance technique training. Let us not feel threatened or intimidated, because as good leaders, we know that all joints can supply. Please show us how to be more inclusive, and not reject others. Let us not be so familiar with one another that we lose sight of what others have to offer. Remind us that we all are part of the body of Christ, and we will function in one accord.

In Jesus' name.

Amen.

EPILOGUE

I realize that some of the topics discussed in this book may not be popular or agreeable, or perhaps they even struck a nerve. I considered this before writing, and if there are blinders pertaining to what was discussed, I believe God asked me to help as He removes the scales from our eyes if they are being covered. The purpose of the intent of this book was not to hurt or to anger but to enlighten, share information and resources, and be prayerful. It was important to share why skill is important to the dance minister, what the benefits are, and what God has to say about it. I believe some people have experienced some of what I have written here, whether as a leader or a team member and may not have felt comfortable enough or had the opportunity to discuss or address them. I pray there will be a more open dialogue between each other and, most importantly, understanding with results.

As dance ministers, we are God's living epistles walking on the earth and have been called to do His will, spread His Word, and show His love without conditions or preferences. There is value and importance in what we do for the Lord, and we are to do it without any hindrances and always in spirit and in truth. As God's dance ministers, we are first His worshippers and then dancers: something He has created and a gift He has given us. We appreciate this, and to further show our appreciation, we are going to take care of this gift, enhance it, and share it in excellence.

As we have been called to dance and move for the Lord, we must strive to work on our natural bodies – our temple, which ministers in God's temple: rest, exercise, healthy diet, and technical dance training. The natural (technique) and the supernatural (prophetic dance) are all one; they go hand in hand and are completely and divinely connected.

We should always earnestly embrace our gift of dance, and the gift of dance in others. We must recognize that it is a gift from God and that it needs to be cultivated with a high level of commitment that includes a purposeful Christian lifestyle: prayer, meditation, supplication, intercession, fasting, praise, and worship.

Let us know the value of each other and know that we are all His creation, and that we can share our gift and knowledge of dance, prophetic and technical, and show each other love. We are servants, and we must humble ourselves to do the work of the ministry and not forget that we are ministering not only to others in the congregation when we move, but also to those we move alongside; we must also serve in love. We should never discount anyone's level of experience in dance, whether they have dance experience or not, and if we have dance technical experience, we should value and welcome that knowledge as well. We should be sharing what we know with one another to help build each other up as we work side by side together, sharing the gospel of Jesus Christ with the world.

REFERENCES

1 Cleveland Clinic, "Heart," https://my.clevelandclinic.org/health/body/21704-heart.

2 Dr. Greg, "Cardiology: The Spiritual Heart Series – Part I: Anatomy & Physiology of the Heart," Everlasting Strength, https://www.everlastingstrength.org/cardiology-the-spiritual-heart-series-part-i-anatomy-physiology-of-the-heart.

3 "Excuse," The Oxford Pocket Dictionary of Current English, https://www.encyclopedia.com/social-sciences-and-law/law/law/excuse.

4 Frank Ocean, https://www.goodreads.com/quotes/7319506-excuses-are-the-tools-of-the-weak-and-incompetent-they.

5 Definitions from Bing Dictionary Online.

6 "Passion," Merriam-Webster, https://www.merriam-webster.com/dictionary/passion.

7 "Technique," Britannica Dictionary, https://www.britannica.com/dictionary/technique.

8 Pamela Hardy, *Dance: The Higher Call: God's Glorious Mandate for Transforming Your Life, Reflecting His Son and Revealing His Glory* (Reignaissance Publications, 2015).

9 Oprah Winfrey, https://www.goodreads.com/quotes/1317721-follow-your-passion-it-will-lead-you-to-your-purpose.

10 "8 Benefits of Dance," *Healthline*, https://www.healthline.com/health/fitness-exercise/benefits-of-dance.

11 Miss Robin Irey Marchiori, "Why Is Studying Dance Technique Important?," October 12, 2014, https://web.archive.org/web/20230329073116/https://www.cgpac.com/cgpac-fyi/why-is-studying-dance-technique-important.

12 "Technique," Dictionary.com, https://www.dictionary.com/browse/technique.

13 "Seek," Dictionary.com, https://www.dictionary.com/browse/seek.

ENDORSEMENT

By: Minister Alicia Siryon-Wells

My relationship with the author, Gina Emanuel-Satchell, began with our shared love for the Horton technique. Flat backs, lateral stretches, primitive squats, lunges, and isolations – all challenging, but our passion for learning this style of technique then transformed into wanting to teach it. Not just to show that we know it, but to help others develop their dance vocabulary and move with more freedom. Gina's desire to share in her technique knowledge ultimately allowed her to birth this informative and timely book, *The Dance Minister and Dance Technique: What God Says About Skill*.

This book allows us to see the reasons why studying and improving our movements through dance technique is so vital to God's Kingdom and why some may not comprehend this concept. The readings will check your heart, your motives, and your why. As dance ministers, more specifically ministers of the gospel, it is imperative to know that God wants us to share His message visually and that His message must be clear! It is time to expand our knowledge, our dance vocabulary, and the way we tell God's story! It is time to get trained!

Minister Alicia Siryon-Wells
National Liturgical Dance Network (NLDN)
State Leader: Massachusetts and Rhode Island
nldnmassachusetts@gmail.com
https://linktr.ee/NLDNMAR

ACKNOWLEDGMENTS

I would like to acknowledge the following dance teachers and dance ministry leaders, who played a huge part in influencing and developing me into the dancer and dance minister I am today:

DANCE EDUCATION:
La-Cher-Tari Dance Studio, Philadelphia, PA
Founder: Cheryl Gaines-Jenkins Teachers: Cheryl Gaines-Jenkins, John Hines, Syreeta Haywood

HIGH SCHOOL FOR CREATIVE AND PERFORMING ARTS (CAPA), PHILADELPHIA, PA
Teachers: LaDeva Davis, Althea Leslie (Hilsendager), John Hines, Scott Schultz, Judith Oruska, Victoria Seitchick, Skeeter

DANCE MINISTRY:
Eagles International Training Institute (EITI)
TEN Worldwide (The Eagles Network)
Founder: Dr. Pamela Hardy, Apostle

TEN Worldwide Director: Apostle Katrina Carter
EITI Choregeo Director: Pastor Janine Dailey, Apostle
Moves of God International: Dr. Sumaya White, Apostle
Mentor: Pastor Carmen Curry

SPECIAL ACKNOWLEDGMENT

April Voltz

I am grateful for your belief in my calling to minister in dance at a time when hardly anyone had dance ministries in the Springfield, Massachusetts area. When we would have special presentations and when you spoke at women's meetings, I appreciated how you would ask me to minister in dance before you spoke. You saw something in me that God used to help mend broken hearts and heal through my movement. That has always meant the world to me.

Thank you.

MANY BLESSINGS TO MY CHURCH FAMILY:
Rafael Luis and Chaquira Osorio, Senior Pastors
Crossover Church, Springfield, MA

Apostles Pedro R. and Loyda Osorio
Iglesia Apostolica Renovación (IAR) Network

My greatest supporter and very best friend, Kyle D. Morris Sr.

THE DANCE MINISTER AND DANCE TECHNIQUE

www.ingramcontent.com/pod-product-compliance
Lightning Source LLC
Chambersburg PA
CBHW071730090426
42738CB00011B/2445